great songs... of folk music

edited by milton okun

ISBN-13: 978-1-57560-952-2
ISBN-10: 1-57560-952-5

Copyright © 2007 Cherry Lane Music Company
International Copyright Secured   All Rights Reserved

Visit our website at www.cherrylane.com

INTRODUCTION

Like the blues, folk music is a genre of the people, by the people, and for the people. Although it periodically goes out of fashion, it will never entirely perish from the earth, simply because the songs are too plentiful, too memorable, and, for its adherents, too meaningful. At times of social and emotional unrest and political ferment, folk songs always address the important issues of the day. If they've been largely absent from the record charts since 1963, they are in the air nonetheless, as troubadours from Pete Seeger to Bob Dylan to John Denver to Bruce Springsteen arise to give them voice at the barricades of change. If all you know of folk music is singing "Kumbaya" around the campfire at summer camp, this book will be an enlightening experience. If you're already well versed in the folk repertoire, it will offer one of the most comprehensive collections available.

The last really commercial moment for folk music was probably its first. Thought of now in varying degrees of fondness, nostalgia, sympathy, or rage as The Great Urban Folk Scare, it was launched by the Weavers in 1950, reawakened by the Kingston Trio in 1958, and brought to the vast, hungry Baby Boom audience just entering college by Peter, Paul & Mary in 1963, with some help from Bob Dylan and Joan Baez. For these earnest, activist Boomers, it was a way to separate themselves from their heathen rock-and-roll counterparts, still twisting the night away. For Pete Seeger, one of the original Weavers, it meant redemption. For Bob Dylan, it was a path to immortality.

If Elvis Presley was censored from the waist down by the lords of television in 1956, the Weavers of 1950 (including Lee Hays, Ronnie Gilbert, Fred Hellerman, as well as Seeger) were censored from the waist up, effectively banned from the public eye for the views they espoused with their hearts and minds. Yet, with their version of Leadbelly's "Goodnight, Irene" ensconced at the top of the charts for 13 weeks in 1950, the Folk Scare was upon us. From the Weavers repertoire came future folk standards like "If I Had a Hammer," "Kisses Sweeter Than Wine" and "Sloop John B," with Pete himself adding the rousing "Guantanamera," the biblical "Turn! Turn! Turn!," the pacifistic "Where Have All the Flowers Gone?," and Woody Guthrie's stirring answer to Irving Berlin's "God Bless America," "This Land Is Your Land," to the volatile mix.

By the late '50s, when folk music made a brief return to the charts, its presentation and acceptance was considered much less subversive. "Tom Dooley," the San Francisco–based Kingston Trio's breakthrough number, dated from the Civil War and was about a double-crossed soldier. Later, their "M.T.A." took on Boston politics. Within a couple of years, folk groups would be in vogue; in matching cardigan sweaters, they were the essence of collegiate, in the fraternity sorority sense. The Highwaymen, from Connecticut's Wesleyan University, brought their clean and articulate harmonies to the old slave song "Michael Row the Boat Ashore" and hit the top of the charts. Clear across the country, the Brothers Four, from the University of Washington, sang the ecologically prescient "Greenfields." Also from the Washington area, the Chad Mitchell Trio proved to be one of the more adventurous of the folk groups, singing songs about the John Birch Society and Lizzie Borden. But their most enduring claim to fame was in their superior choice of a replacement for the departing Chad, the great John Denver, who would go on to interpret and contribute many songs to the folk canon, among them "Follow Me" and "Sunshine on My Shoulders."

In New York City, folk music became a career move, as Erik Darling, former lead banjo player of the Tarriers, recruited a Benny Goodman vocalist and a local guitarist for his new group, the Rooftop Singers, and turned Gus Cannon's 1929 jug band ditty "Walk Right In" into a number one hit. As if cast for a Broadway show, solo artist Peter Yarrow, former stand-up comic Paul Stookey, and fledgling actress Mary Travers were constructed by impresario Albert Grossman, instructed in the niceties of vocalizing, and provided with the best of material, from Will Holt's "Lemon Tree" to the Yarrow-Lipton gem "Puff the Magic Dragon," to the earliest works of another Grossman discovery, Bob Dylan.

When Dylan arrived in Greenwich Village in New York City in 1961, it wasn't as if he put the place on the map. Folk singers and other bohemian types had been flocking to the Village all century. But Dylan had studied the masters well, from Woody Guthrie, Pete Seeger, Hank Williams, and Buddy Holly, to, if you believe his autobiography, Bobby Vee. His alliance with Joan Baez was as fortunate as it was legendary. Joan was going the way of the old wave when Dylan met her, a Harvard Square nightingale, singing serious ballads like "All My Trials" and "We Shall Overcome." Although Dylan started out on his first album singing ballads too in a very unBaez-like holler, among them "House of the Rising Sun" and "Man of Constant Sorrow," pretty soon he was mirroring his generation in defiance of the prescribed, proscribed agenda, with songs of his own: "Blowing in the Wind" and "Don't Think Twice, It's All Right," both commercially covered in the Top 10 by Peter, Paul & Mary.

As Dylan's progress touched a nerve in the rampant, raging collegiate audience, soon to be the dropout Alternate Culture, his creative drive and output was a goad to his peers, who began writing too, many of them out of the same Gaslight cafe headquarters, down a flight of stairs on Macdougal Street. Here were your protest singer/songwriter journalists like Phil Ochs ("There but for Fortune," "I Ain't Marching Anymore) and Buffy Sainte-Marie ("Universal Soldier"), and the novelist Leonard Cohen ("Suzanne"). Here were your modern troubadours like the prolific and poignant Tom Paxton, summing up his peers and his generation in anthems like "I Can't Help but Wonder (Where I'm Bound)" and "My Ramblin' Boy."

Those boys and girls have rambled on since then, replaced by others in the ceaseless parade. Whoever else with plans to join them should study the works in this book as sacred text, in preparation for the next wave.

—Bruce Pollock

Bruce Pollock is the author of *When the Music Mattered: Rock in the 1960s* and *The Rock Song Index: The 7500 Most Important Songs of the Rock and Roll Era, 1944-2000.*

CONTENTS

All My Trials

Adapted and Arranged by Peter Yarrow,
Noel Stookey and Milt Okun

7

Blowin' In The Wind

Words and Music by Bob Dylan

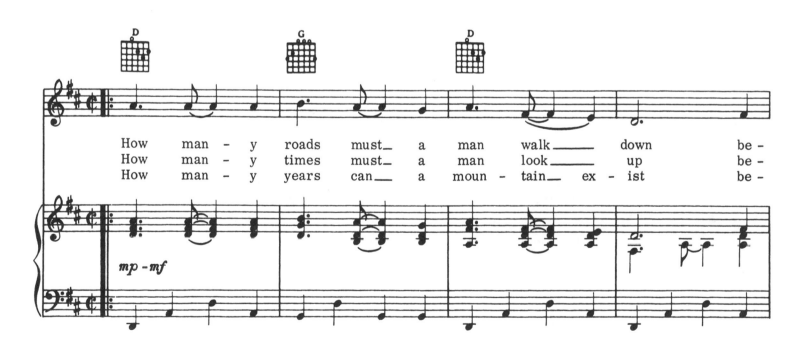

How man—y roads must_ a man walk_____ down be-
How man—y times must_ a man look_____ up be-
How man—y years can_ a moun-tain_ ex-ist be-

fore   you call him a   man?_____ Yes,__ 'n'
fore he__ can see the_____   sky?_____ Yes,__ 'n'
fore it's washed to__ the   sea?_____ Yes,__ 'n'

how man - y seas must__ a   white dove_____
how man - y ears must__ one   man_____
how man - y years can__ some peo - ple__ ex -

sail   be - fore   she sleeps in____ the
have   be - fore he__ can hear peo - ple
ist   be - fore they're__ al - lowed to____ be

9

sand? _____ Yes,_ 'n' how man - y times must_ the
cry? _____ Yes,_ 'n' how man - y deaths will_ it
free? _____ Yes,_ 'n' how man - y times can_ a

can - non balls _____ fly be - fore they're _____
take ___ till ___ he knows that too man - y
man ___ turn ___ his head pre - tend - ing ___ he

for - ev - er banned? _____
peo - ple ___ er have died? _____   The
just does - n't see? _____

Bottle Of Wine

Words and Music by Tom Paxton

Additional Lyrics

2. It's a little hotel, older than hell,
   And as dark as the coal in the mine.
   The blankets are thin, I lay there and grin,
   'Cause I've got a little bottle of wine. *(To Chorus)*

3. It's a pain in my head, and bugs in my bed,
   And my pants are so old that they shine.
   Out on the street, tell the people I meet,
   "Won't you buy me a bottle of wine?" *(To Chorus)*

4. A preacher will preach, and a teacher will teach,
   And a miner will dig in the mine.
   I ride the rods, trusting in God,
   And huggin' my bottle of wine. *(To Chorus)*

Dona Dona

Words and Music by Sholom Sholem Secunda,
Sheldon Secunda, Teddi Schwartz,
Arthur Kevess and Aaron Zeitlin

Note: Chord names in parentheses represent chords played by guitar capoed at the 7th fret.

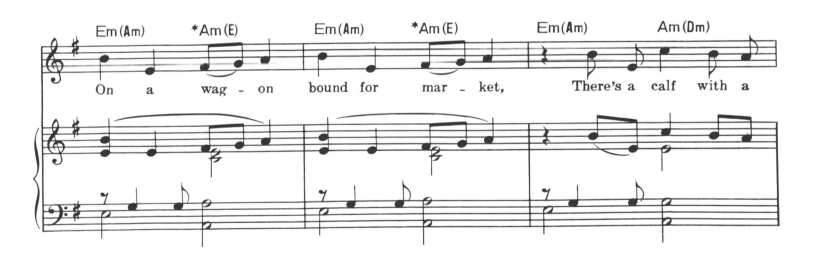

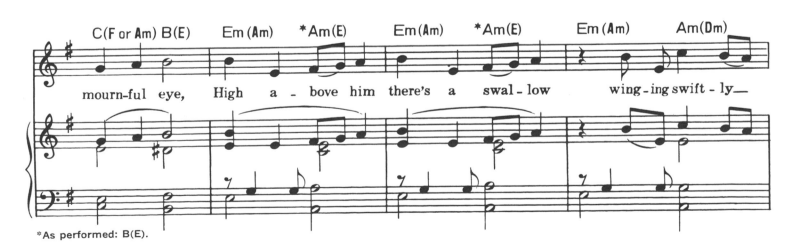

*As performed: B(E).

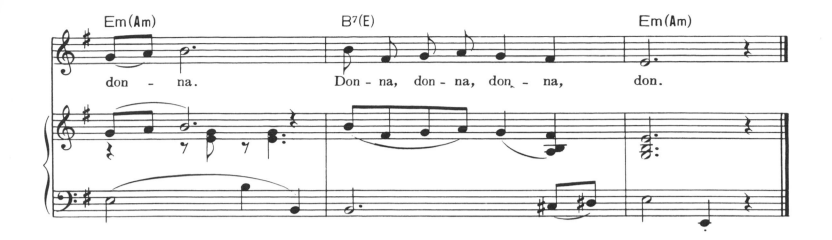

don - na.   Don - na, don - na, don - na,   don.

2. "Stop complaining," said the farmer, "Who told you a calf to be,
    Why don't you have wings to fly with, like the swallow so proud and free?"
    How the winds are laughing, they laugh with all their might,
    Laugh and laugh the whole day through, and half the Summer's night.

    Donna, Donna, Donna, Donna; Donna, Donna, Donna, Don——— (2)

3. Calves are easily bound and slaughtered, never knowing the reason why,
    But whoever treasures freedom, like the swallow has learned to fly,
    How the winds are laughing, they laugh with all their might,
    Laugh and laugh the whole day through, and half the Summer's night.

    Donna, etc.

Catch The Wind

Words and Music by Donovan Leitch

1. In the chil - ly hours and
(Verses 2 & 3 see block lyric)

mi - nutes of un - cer - tain - ty.

I want to be in the warm hold of your lov - ing mind. To feel you all a - round me and to take your hand a - long the sand, ah, but I may as well

⊕ Coda

Verse 2:
When sundown pales the sky
I want to hide awhile
Behind your smile
And everywhere I'd look, your eyes I'd find.

For me to love you now
Would be the sweetest thing
'Twould make me sing
Ah but I may as well try and catch the wind.

Verse 3:
When rain has hung the leaves with tears
I want you near
To kill my fears
To help me leave all my blues behind

For standing in your heart
Is where I want to be
And I long to be
Ah but I may as well try and catch the wind.

Day-O (The Banana Boat Song)

Words and Music by
Irving Burgie and William Attaway

Moderate Calypso

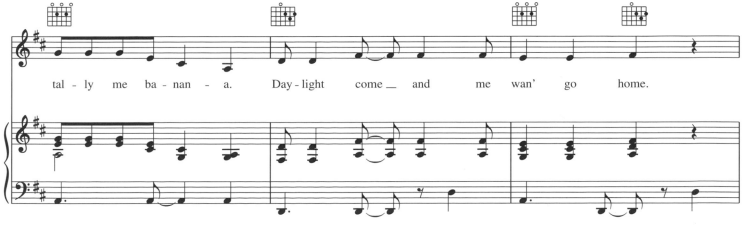

Work all night — on a drink of rum. — Day - light come — and me wan' go home. Stack ba - nan - a till de morn - ing come. — Day - light come — and me wan' go home. Come, Mis - ter tal - ly man, tal - ly me ba - nan - a. Day - light come — and me wan' go home.

27

Don't Think Twice, It's All Right

Words and Music by Bob Dylan

now.   When the   roost - er   crows   at the   break   of
road.   Still I   wish there   was   some-thin' you would   do   or

dawn   Look out your   win-dow and   I'll   be   gone.
say   To try and   make me change my   mind   and   stay.

You're   the   rea-son I'm   trav-'lin' an-y -   on   Don't think
We nev - er   did too much talk-in' an-y -   way   So don't think

twice, it's all   right.   2. It   right.   3. I'm
(4. It)

walk-in' down that long lone-some road, Babe
ain't no use in call-in' out my name, Gal

Where I'm bound I can't tell But
Like you nev-er did be-fore It

good-bye's too good a word, Gal
ain't no use in call-in' out my name, Gal

So I'll just say fare thee well.
I can't say hear you an-y more. I ain't
I'm a-

say - in' and   you treat - ed   me   un - kind   You
think - in' and a - won-d'rin' all the   way   down the   road   I

could have   done   bet - ter _____ but   I   don't   mind.
once   loved a   wom - an _____ a   child I'm   told.   I

You just kind-a   wast-ed   my pre - cious   time.   But don't think
give   her my   heart but she want-ed   my   soul.   But don't think

twice,   It's all   right.   4. It
twice,   It's all   right.

Five Hundred Miles

Words and Music by Hedy West

Moderately slow

If you miss the train I'm on, you will know that I am gone; you can hear the whis-tle blow _____ a hun-dred miles. _____

Follow Me

Words and Music by John Denver

Moderately fast

It's by far the hard-est thing ___ I've ev-er done, ___ To be so in love with you and so a - lone. ___

*Guitarists: Tune lowest string to D.

Fol - low me____ where I go,____ what I do____ ____ and who I know,_____ Make it part of you____ to be a part of me._____ Fol-low me__

up and down,___ all ___ the way and all a - round,.

Take my hand ___ and say you'll fol - low me. ___

It's long been on my mind,.
You see, I'd like to share my life ___

just how much I need you ___ To be there where I can
nev - er be a - lone ___ and all the time that

talk to you when there's no one else a - round. ___
you're with me, then we will be at home. ___

Coda

way. ___

Take my hand __ and

say you'll fol - low me. ___

Greenfields

Words and Music by Terry Gilkyson,
Richard Dehr and Frank Miller

Slowly, with a steady beat

Guantanamera

Musical Adaptation by Pete Seeger and Julian Orbon
Lyric Adaptation by Julian Orbon, based on a poem by Jose Marti
Lyric Editor: Hector Angulo
Original Music and Lyrics by Jose Fernandez Diaz

Verse:

1. Yo soy un hom - bre sin - ce - ro   De don - de

cre - ce la pal - ma   Yo soy un hom - bre sin - ce - ro

de don - de cre - ce la pal - ma   Y an - tes de

mo - rir - me quie - ro   E - char mis ver - sos del al - ma.

2. Mi verso es de un verde claro
   Y de un carmin encendido
   Mi verso es de un verde claro
   Y de un carmin encendido
   Mi verso es un cierro herido
   Que busca en el monte amparo.
   (Chorus)

3. Con los pobres de la tierra
   Quiero yo mi suerte echar
   Con los pobres de la tierra
   Quiero yo mi suerte echar
   El arroyo de la sierra
   Me complace mas que el mar.
   (Chorus)

(Literal English Translation)

1. I am a truthful man, from the
   land of palm trees. Before
   dying, I want to share these
   poems of my soul.

2. My poems are light green,
   but they are also flaming
   crimson. My verses are like
   a wounded faun, seeking
   refuge in the forest.

3. With the poor people of this
   earth, I want to share my fate.
   The little streams of the
   mountains please me more
   than the sea.

The House Of The Rising Sun

Words and Music by Alan Price

Slowly and steadily

Spend   your   lives ____ in sin and ____ mis - er - y _____ in the

house _____ of the Ris - ing Sun.

Well, ___ I've got   one   foot   on   the
                      is   a   house   in

I Ain't Marching Anymore

Words and Music by Phil Ochs

Oh, I marched to the Bat - tle of ___
stole Cal - i - for - nia from the
flew the fi - nal mis - sion in the

New Or - leans at the end of the
Mex - i - can land, fought in the
Jap - an - ese skies, set off the

ear - ly Brit - ish wars.
blood - y Civ - il War. Yes, I
might - y mush - room roar. When I

young land start - ed grow - ing, the young blood start - ed
e - ven killed my broth - ers, and so man - y
saw the cit - ies burn - ing, I knew that I was

flow - ing, but I ain't a - march - ing an - y -
oth - ers, but I ain't a - march - ing an - y -
learn - ing that I ain't a - march - ing an - y -

man - y more a - dy - ing,
now they want me back a - gain,
love or call it rea - son,
but I ain't a - march - ing an - y - more!

It's al - ways the old to lead us to the wars, al - ways the young to fall.

Now look at all we've won with a sa - ber and a

I Can't Help But Wonder (Where I'm Bound)

Words and Music by Tom Paxton

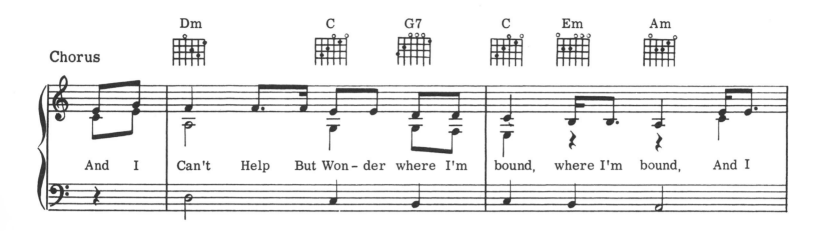

Chorus

And I Can't Help But Won-der where I'm bound, where I'm bound, And I

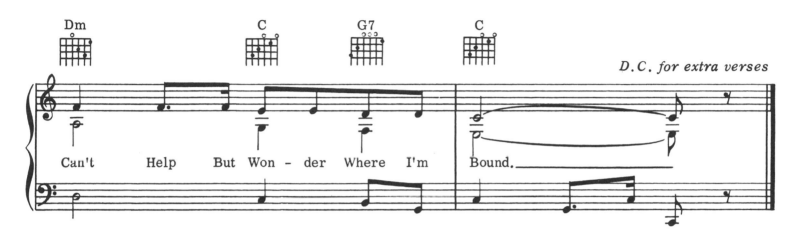

D.C. for extra verses

Can't Help But Won - der Where I'm Bound._____

Additional Verses

2. I have been around this land
   Just a-doin' the best I can
   Tryin' to find what I was meant to do.
   And the faces that I see
   Are as worried as can be
   And it looks like they are wonderin' too.
   (Chorus)

3. I had a little gal one time
   She had lips like sherry wine
   And she loved me till my head went plumb insane
   But I was too blind to see
   She was driftin' away from me
   And one day she left on the morning train.
   (Chorus)

4. I've got a buddy from home
   But he started out to roam
   And I hear he's out by Frisco Bay
   And sometimes when I've had a few
   His voice comes singin' through
   And I'm goin' out to see him some old day
   (Chorus)

5. If you see me passing by
   And you sit and wonder why
   And you wish that you were a rambler, too,
   Nail your shoes to the kitchen floor
   Lace 'em up and bar the door
   Thank your stars for the roof that's over you.
   (Chorus)

I'll Never Find Another You

Words and Music by Tom Springfield

There's a new world some-where they call the prom-ised land ___ and I'll be there some-day if you will hold my hand. ___ I still need you there be-side ___ me no

al - ways some-one they for each of us they say ___ and you'll be my some-one if ev - er and a day. ___ I could search the whole world o - ver un-

Jamaica Farewell

Words and Music by Irving Burgie

If I Had A Hammer (The Hammer Song)

Words and Music by Lee Hays and Pete Seeger

from the Motion Picture A MIGHTY WIND

A Kiss At The End Of The Rainbow

Words and Music by Michael John McKean and Annette O'Toole

Oh, when the veil of dreams has lift-ed and the fair-y tales have all been told, there's a kiss ___ at the end of the rain-

Your kiss... There's a kiss ___ at the end ___ of the

rain - bow   more   pre - cious than a   pot   of   gold.

Kum Ba Yah

Traditional Spiritual

Kisses Sweeter Than Wine

Words by Ronnie Gilbert, Lee Hays, Fred Hellerman and Pete Seeger
Music by Huddie Ledbetter

Verse

1. When I was a young man and nev-er been kissed, I got to
(*Verses 2-5 see block lyric*)

think-in' o-ver what I had missed. I got me a girl I

kissed her and then, Oh, Lord, I kissed her a-gain.

D.%. al Fine

Verse 2:
He asked me to marry and be his sweet wife,
And we would be so happy all of our life.
He begged and he pleaded like a natural man and then,
Oh, Lord, I gave him my hand. *(Repeat chorus)*

Verse 3:
I worked mighty hard and so did my wife,
A-workin' hand in hand to make a good life.
With corn in the fields and wheat in the bins and then,
Oh, Lord, I was the father of twins. *(Repeat chorus)*

Verse 4:
Our children numbered just about four
And they all had sweethearts knock on the door.
They all got married and they didn't wait, I was,
Oh, Lord, the grandfather of eight. *(Repeat chorus)*

Verse 5:
Now we are old and ready to go
We get to thinkin' what happened a long time ago.
We had lots of kids and trouble and pain, but,
Oh, Lord, we'd do it again. *(Repeat chorus)*

Lemon Tree

Words and Music by Will Holt

les - son from the love - ly lem - on tree." "Don't
when she smiled the stars rose in the sky. We
left be - hind I knew what she had done. She'd

put your faith in love, my boy," my fa - ther said to me. "I
passed that sum - mer lost in love be - neath the lem - on tree. The
left me for an - oth - er, it's a com - mon tale, but true. A

fear you'll find that love is like the love - ly, lem - on tree. Lem - on
mu - sic of her laugh - ter hid my fa - ther's words from me. Lem - on
sad - der man but wis - er now, I sing these words to you.

chorus:

poco rit.

tree ver - y pret - ty, and the lem - on flow - er is

sweet. But the fruit of the poor lem - on is im -

pos - si - ble to eat. Lem - on tree ver - y

pret - ty, and the lem - on flow - er is sweet. But the

Man Of Constant Sorrow

Music by Noel Stookey and Peter Yarrow

The Marvelous Toy

Words and Music by Tom Paxton

The M.T.A.

Words and Music by Jacqueline Steiner and Bess Hawes

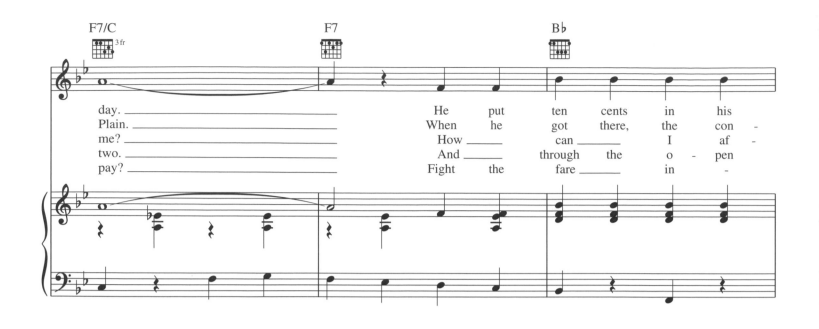

day. _____ He put ten cents in his
Plain. _____ When he got there, the con -
me? _____ How _____ can _____ I af -
two. _____ And _____ through the o - pen
pay? _____ Fight the fare _____ in -

pock - et, kissed his wife _____ and fam - 'ly, went to
duc - tor told him, "One and more nick - el." Char - lie
ford to see my sis - ter in Chel - sea, or my
win - dow she hands Char - lie a sand - wich as the
crease, _____ Fight the fare in - crease, _____ get _____

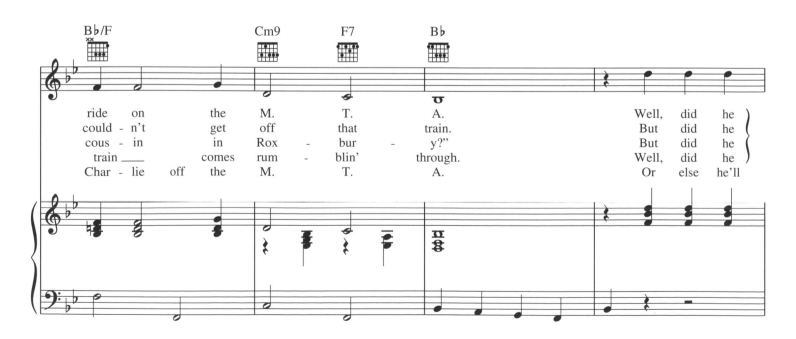

ride on the M. T. A. Well, did he
could - n't get off that train. But did he
cous - in in Rox - bur - y?" But did he
train _____ comes rum - blin' through. Well, did he
Char - lie off the M. T. A. Or else he'll

Michael Row The Boat Ashore

Traditional Folksong

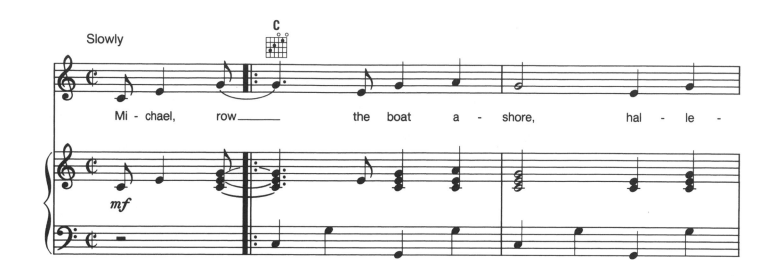

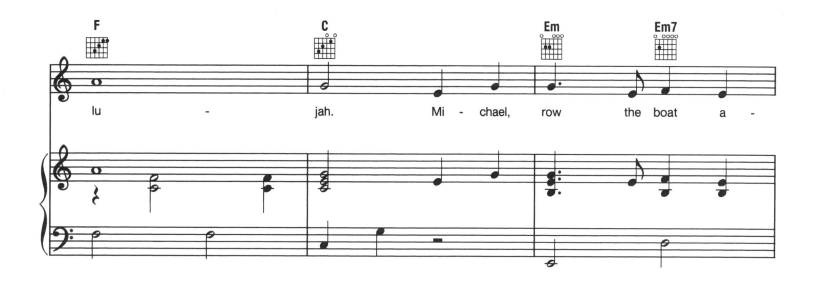

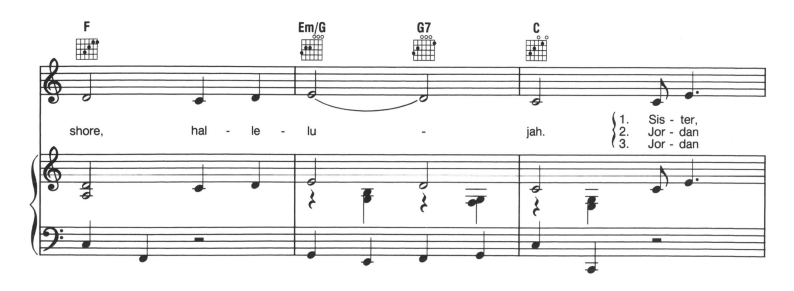

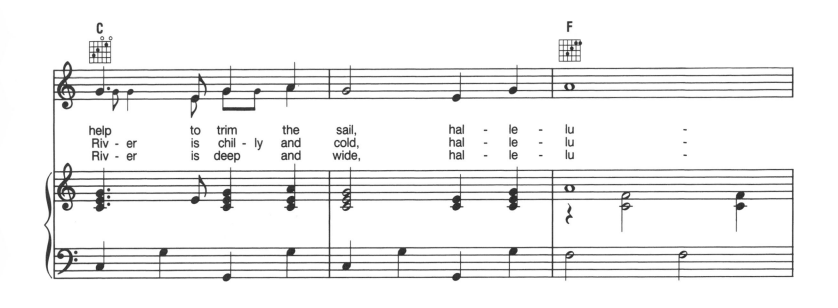

help   to   trim   the   sail,   hal - le - lu -

Riv - er   is chil - ly and   cold,   hal - le - lu -

Riv - er   is deep   and   wide,   hal - le - lu -

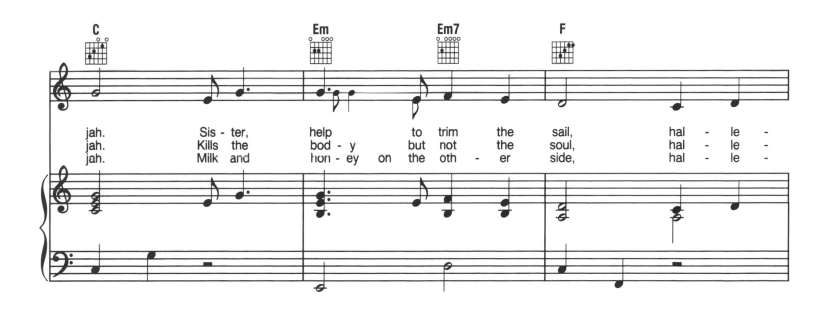

jah.   Sis - ter,   help   to   trim   the   sail,   hal - le -

jah.   Kills the   bod - y but not   the   soul,   hal - le -

jah.   Milk and hon - ey on the oth - er   side,   hal - le -

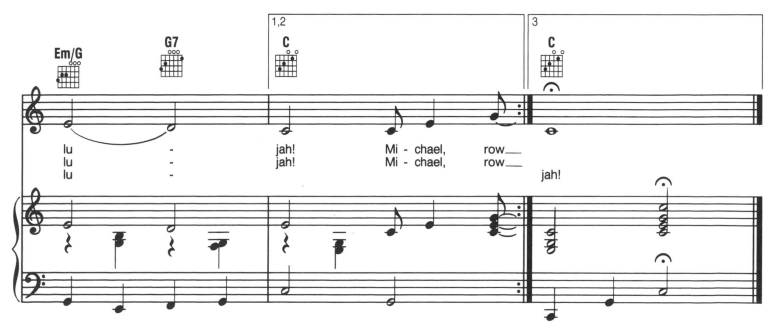

lu -   jah!   Mi - chael,   row___

lu -   jah!   Mi - chael,   row___

lu -   jah!

My Ramblin' Boy

Words and Music by Tom Paxton

G7　　　　　　　　　　　C

me＿＿＿＿＿ in the hard old days＿＿＿＿＿ He nev-er　cared＿＿＿ if I had no
try＿＿＿＿＿ to　work one　day＿＿＿＿＿ The boss said　he＿＿＿ had　room for

G7　　　　　　　　　　　C　　　　　　　　　Chorus:

dough＿＿＿＿ We ram-bled 'round＿＿＿ in the rain and　snow.＿＿＿＿ } And here's to
one＿＿＿＿ Says my old　pal,＿＿＿ "We'd rath-er　bum!"＿＿＿

C　　　F　　C　　　　　　　　　　G7

you,＿＿＿ my ram-blin'　boy,＿＿＿ May all your　ram - blin' bring you

89

ADDITIONAL VERSES

3. Late one night in a jungle camp
    The weather it was cold and damp
    He got the chills and he got 'em bad
    They took the only friend I had.
    (Chorus)

4. He left me there to ramble on
    My ramblin' pal is dead and gone
    If when we die we go somewhere
    I'll bet you a dollar he's ramblin' there.
    (Chorus to final ending)

Sloop John B

Words and Music by Brian Wilson

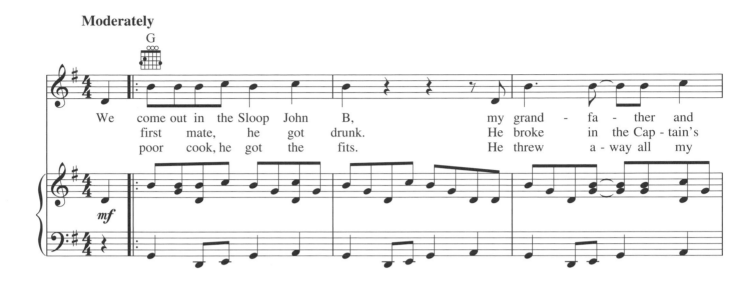

got in - to a fight.
why don't you leave me a - lone?
Why don't they let me go home?

Well, I
Well, I
This

feel so broke up
feel so broke up
is the worst trip

I wan - na go home.
I wan - na go home.
I've ev - er been on.

So hoist up the John B sail,

see how the main sail set. Call for the Cap - tain a -

shore. Let me go home, let ___ me go

home. I wan - na go home, oh

yeah. Well, I feel so broke ___ up I wan - na go

1, 2 home.

3 The home. _____

Puff The Magic Dragon

Words and Music by Lenny Lipton and Peter Yarrow

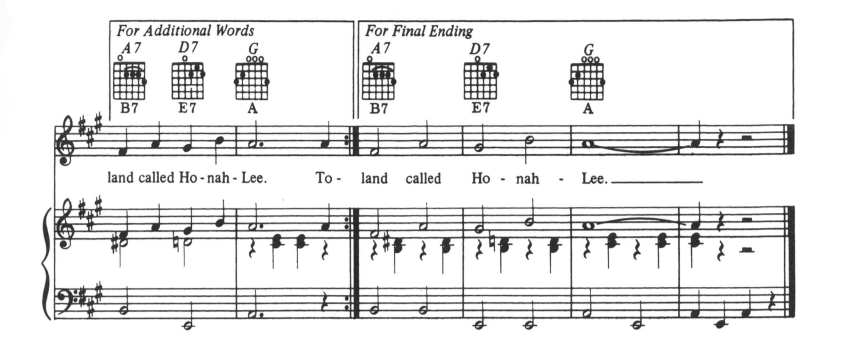

land called Ho-nah-Lee.   To-   land   called   Ho-   nah - Lee. _____

ADDITIONAL WORDS

2. Together they would travel on a boat with billowed sail,
    Jackie kept a lookout perched on Puff's gigantic tail,
    Noble kings and princes would bow whene'er they came,
    Pirate ships would low'r their flag when Puff roared out his name. Oh!
    (Chorus)

3. A dragon lives forever but not so little boys,
    Painted wings and giant rings make way for other toys.
    One grey night it happened, Jackie Paper came no more
    And Puff that mighty dragon, he ceased his fearless roar. Oh!
    (Chorus)

4. His head was bent in sorrow, green scales fell like rain,
    Puff no longer went to play along the cherry lane.
    Without his life-long friend, Puff could not be brave
    So Puff that mighty dragon, sadly slipped into his cave. Oh!
    (Chorus)

Scarborough Fair/Canticle

Arrangement and Original Counter Melody by Paul Simon and Arthur Garfunkel

Re - mem - ber

me   to   one who lives   there. _____

She   once was   a   true love of mine. _____

Ahead to next strain

Fine

mine.

rit.

p

bed - clothes the child of the moun - tain.
cleans and po - lish -es a gun.
cause they've long a - go for - got - ten.

work, _____ Then she'll be a true love of
strands, _____ Then she'll be a true love of
heath - er, _____ Then she'll be a true love of

1.2.

Sleeps un - a - ware of the clar - i - on call.

mine. _____
mine. _____

3.

D.S. al Fine

mine. _____

Sunshine On My Shoulders

Words by John Denver
Music by John Denver, Mike Taylor and Dick Kniss

song that I could sing for you,____   I'd
wish that I could wish for you,____   I'd

Last time, D.S. % al ⊕ Coda

sing a song____ to make you feel this way.____
make a wish____ for sun-shine all the while.____

Coda
⊕

Sun-shine____ al-most all the time makes me high,____

sun-shine____ al-most al-ways...____

104

There But For Fortune

Words and Music by Phil Ochs

Show me a pris - on, _____
Show me an al - ley, _____
Show me the whis - key _____
Show me a coun - try _____

show me a jail.
show me a train.
that stains on the floor.
where the bombs had to fall.

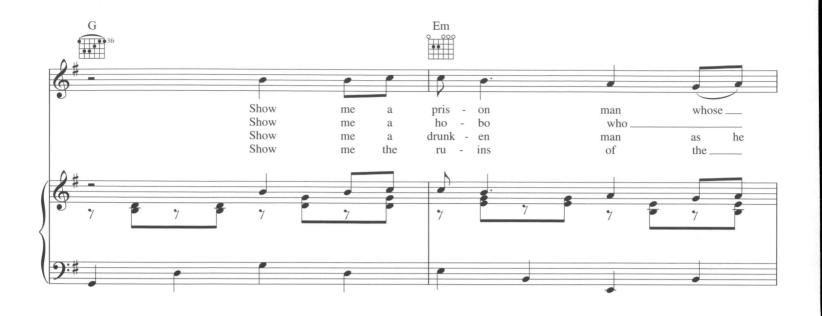

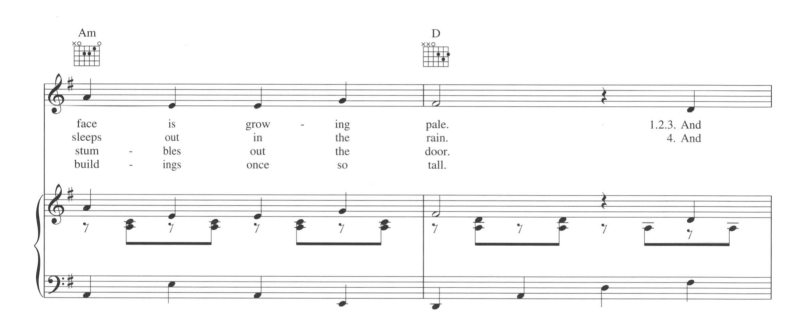

Suzanne

Words and Music by Leonard Cohen

cra - zy and that's why you want to be there; And she
cer - tain on - ly why drown - ing men could see Him He
hon - ey on our la - dy of the har - bour; And she

feeds you tea and o-ran-ges that came all the way from Chi - na, And
said "All men shall be sail - ors, then, un - til the sea shall free them," But
shows you where to look a - mid the gar - bage and the flow - ers. There are

just when you want to tell her___ that you have no love to give her___ she
He Him-self was bro-ken long be-fore the sky would o - pen.___ For -
he - roes in the sea-weed,___ There are chil - dren in the morn-ing,___ they are

109

gets you on her wave length and lets the riv-er an-swer that you've
sak - en, al - most hu - man, He sank be-neath your wis-dom like a
lean-ing out for love, and they will lean that way for - ev - er while

al - ways____ been her lov-er.____ And you
stone._____ And you
Suz - anne____ holds her mir-ror.____ And you

Chorus

want to trav-el with her,____ And you want to trav-el blind,____ And you
want to trav-el with Him,____ And you want to trav-el blind,____ And you
want to trav-el with her,____ And you want to trav-el blind,____ And you

think you may - be trust her,___ 'Cause she's touched your per-fect bod-y,___ with her
think you may - be trust Him,___ For he's touched your per-fect bod-y,___ with His
think may-be you'll trust her,___ For you've touched her per-fect bod-y,___ with your

1.2.

mind._____
mind._____

2. And
3. Suz -

3.

mind._____

ritard

This Land Is Your Land

Words and Music by Woody Guthrie

Bright and cheerfully

low me ___ that gold - en val - ley; ___
for - est ___ to the Gulf Stream wa - ters; ___
round me ___ a voice was sound - ing; ___
lift - ing, ___ a voice was chant - ing: ___

this land was made for you and

me. ___
{ 2.,4.,6. This land is
3. I've roamed and   me. ___
5. Well, the sun came

rit.

Time In A Bottle

Words and Music by Jim Croce

is to save ev - 'ry day 'til e - ter - ni - ty
I'd save ev - 'ry day like a treas - ure and

pass - es a - way just to spend them with you.
then a - gain I would spend them with you.

If
But there nev - er seems to

be e - nough time to do the things you want to do once you

find them. _____ I've

looked a - round e - nough to know that you're the one I want to go through

time with. If

I had a box just for wish es _____ and

dreams that had nev - er come true, _____ the

box would be emp - ty ex - cept for the mem - 'ry of

how they were an - swered by you. _____ But there

CODA

Play 3 times

The Times They Are A-Changin'

Words and Music by Bob Dylan

soon you'll be drenched to the bone, _____ if your

time to you is worth sav - in' _____ then you

bet - ter start swim - min' or you'll sink like a stone, for the

times they are a - chang -

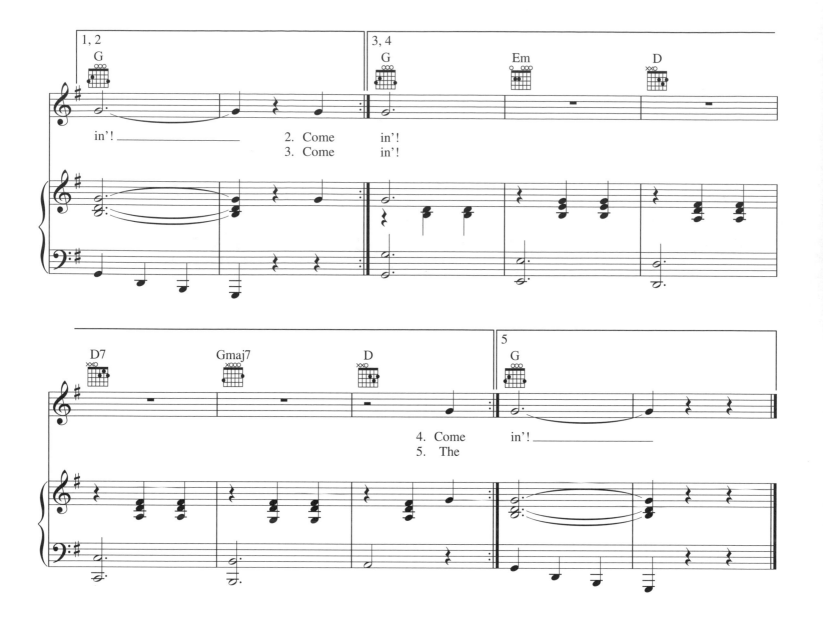

Additional Lyrics

2. Come writers and critics
   Who prophesy with your pen
   And keep your eyes wide
   The chance won't come again.
   And don't speak too soon
   For the wheel's still in spin,
   And there's no tellin' who
   That it's namin'.
   For the loser now
   Will be later to win
   For the times they are a-changin'.

3. Come senators, congressmen
   Please heed the call
   Don't stand in the doorway
   Don't block up the hall.
   For he that gets hurt
   Will be he who has stalled,
   There's a battle
   Outside and it's ragin'.
   It'll soon shake your windows
   And rattle your walls
   For the times they are a-changin'!

4. Come mothers and fathers,
   Throughout the land
   And don't criticize
   What you can't understand.
   Your sons and your daughters
   Are beyond your command,
   Your old road is
   Rapidly agin'.
   Please get out of the new one
   If you can't lend your hand
   For the times they are a-changin'!

5. The line it is drawn
   The curse it is cast
   The slow one now will
   Later be fast.
   As the present now
   Will later be past,
   The order is rapidly fadin'.
   And the first one now
   Will later be last
   For the times they are a-changin'!

We Shall Overcome

Musical and Lyrical Adaptation by Zilphia Horton, Frank Hamilton, Guy Carawan and Pete Seeger
Inspired by African American Gospel Singing, members of the Food and Tobacco Workers Union, Charleston, SC, and the southern Civil Rights Movement

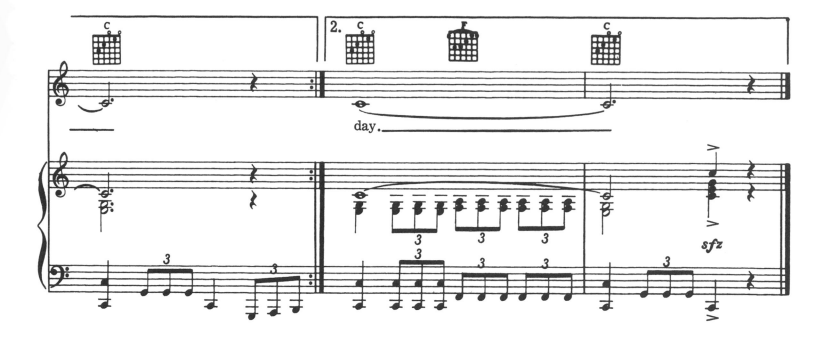

3. We are not afraid, we are not afraid,
   We are not afraid today,
   Oh, deep in my heart I do believe
   We shall overcome some day.

4. We shall stand together, we shall stand together,
   We shall stand together - now,
   Oh, deep in my heart I do believe
   We shall overcome some day.

5. The truth will make us free, the truth will make us free,
   The truth will make us free some day.
   Oh, deep in my heart I do believe
   We shall overcome some day.

6. The Lord will see us through, the Lord will see us through,
   The Lord will see us through some day,
   Oh, deep in my heart I do believe
   We shall overcome some day.

7. We shall be like Him, we shall be like Him,
   We shall be like Him someday,
   Oh, deep in my heart I do believe
   We shall overcome someday.

8. We shall live in peace, we shall live in peace,
   We shall live in peace some day,
   Oh, deep in my heart I do believe
   We shall overcome some day.

9. The whole wide world around, the whole wide world around,
   The whole wide world around some day,
   Oh, deep in my heart I do believe
   We shall overcome some day.

10. We shall overcome, we shall overcome,
    We shall overcome some day,
    Oh, deep in my heart I do believe
    We shall overcome some day.

Tom Dooley

Words and Music Collected, Adapted and Arranged by Frank Warner, John A. Lomax and Alan Lomax
From the singing of Frank Proffitt

met her on the moun - tain And stabbed her with _ my knife.
had-n' - a been for Gray - son I'd - a been in Ten - nes - see.
In some lone - some val - ley A - hang-in' on a white _ oak tree.

Hang down ' your head, Tom Doo - ley, Hang down your head and

cry, Hang down your head, Tom Doo - ley, Poor

boy, you're bound _ to die. die.

Turn Around

Words and Music by Alan Greene,
Malvina Reynolds and Harry Belafonte

Turn! Turn! Turn! (To Everything There Is A Season)

Words from the Book of Ecclesiastes
Adaptation and Music by Pete Seeger

Moderately slow, in 2

The Unicorn

Words and Music by Shel Silverstein

2. Lord seen some sinnin' and it caused him pain,
   He says, "Stand back, I'm gonna make it rain.
   So hey, Brother Noah, I'll tell you what to do,
   Go and build me a floating zoo."
   CHORUS:
   "And you take two alligators and a couple of geese,
   Two hump back camels and two chimpanzees,
   Two cats, two rats, two elephants, but sure as you're born,
   Noah, don't you forget my unicorns."

3. Now Noah was there and he answered the callin'
   And he finished up the ark as the rain started fallin',
   Then he marched in the animals two by two,
   And he sung out as they went through:
   CHORUS:
   "Hey Lord, I got you two alligators and a couple of geese,
   Two hump back camels and two chimpanzees,
   Two cats, two rats, two elephants, but sure as you're born,
   Lord, I just don't see your unicorns."

4. Well, Noah looked out through the drivin' rain,
   But the unicorns was hidin'—— playin' silly games,
   They were kickin' and a-splashin' while the rain was pourin',
   Oh them foolish unicorns.
   CHORUS: Repeat 2nd Chorus

5. Then the ducks started duckin' and the snakes started snakin',
   And the elephants started elephantin' and the boat started shakin',
   The mice started squeakin' and the lions started roarin',
   And everyone's aboard but them unicorns.
   CHORUS:
   I mean the two alligators and a couple of geese,
   The hump back camels and the chimpanzees,
   Noah cried, "Close the door 'cause the rain is pourin',
   And we just can't wait for them unicorns."

6. And then the ark started movin' and it drifted with the tide
   And the unicorns looked up from the rock and cried,
   And the water came up and sort of floated them away,
   That's why you've never seen a unicorn to this day.
   CHORUS:
   You'll see a lot of alligators and a whole mess of geese,
   You'll see hump back camels and chimpanzees,
   You'll see cats and rats and elephants but sure as you're born,
   You're never gonna see no unicorn.

The Universal Soldier

Words and Music by Buffy Saint-Marie

Until It's Time For You To Go

Words and Music by Buffy Sainte-Marie

Moderately fast

You're not a dream, you're not an an-gel, you're a man.
dif-f'rent, worlds a-part, we're not the same,

I'm not a queen, I'm a wom-an, take my hand.
we laughed and played at the start like in a game.

We'll make a space in the lives that we'd planned,
You could have stayed out-side my heart but in you came,

and here we'll stay   un - til it's time   for you to
and here you'll stay   un - til it's time   for you to

go.   Yes, we're go _____

Don't ask ___   why, _____

don't ask ___   how, _____

nev-er in my life see you a-gain,_____ still I'll

stay un-til it's time for you to go._____

Don't ask ___ why of me,

don't ask ___ how of me, _____

don't ask _____ for - ev - er of __ me,
love me, ___ love me ___ now. _____ You're not a
dream, you're not an an - gel, you're a man, _____
___ I'm not a queen, I'm a wom - an, take my

hand. _____ We'll make a space in the

lives that we'd planned, _____ and here we'll

stay un-til it's time for ___ you to go.

molto rit.

a tempo

143

Walk Right In

Words and Music by Gus Cannon and H. Woods

Moderately, with a strong beat

The Water Is Wide

Traditional

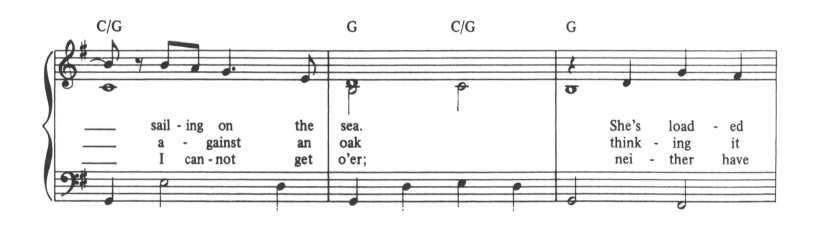

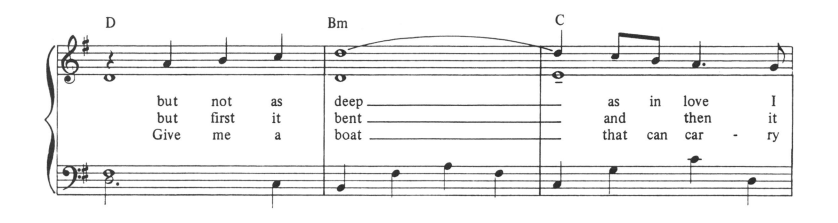

but   not   as   deep _____ as   in   love   I
but   first   it   bent _____ and   then   it
Give   me   a   boat _____ that   can   car - ry

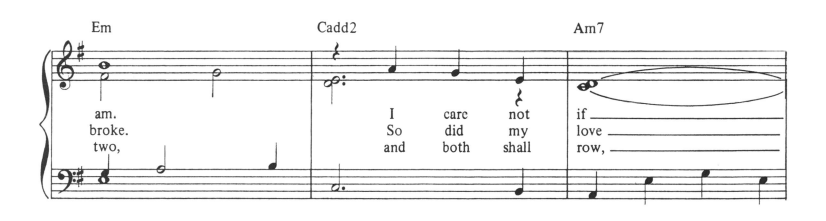

am.   I   care   not   if _____
broke.   So   did   not   my   love _____
two,   and   did   both   shall   row, _____

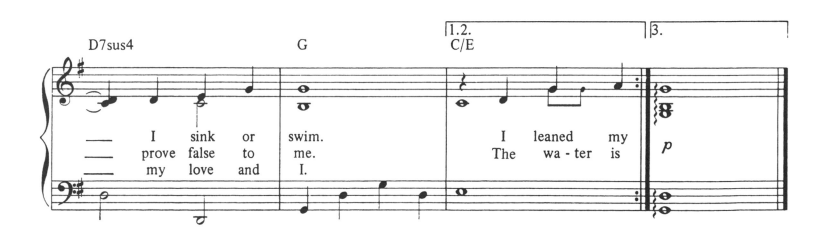

_____   I   sink   or   swim.   I   leaned   my
_____   prove   false   to   me.   The   wa - ter   is
_____   my   love   and   I.   *p*

Wild Mountain Thyme

Traditional Scottish Folksong

1. For the sum-mer-time is com-ing, And the trees are sweet-ly
2. If my true love will not go, I will sure-ly find an-
3. I will build my love a bow-er By yon clear crys-tal

bloom-ing,_ And the wild moun-tain thyme,_ Blooms a - round the pur-ple
oth-er,_ To pull wild moun-tain thyme,_ All a - round the pur-ple
foun-tain, And in it I will pile All the flow - ers from the

With a steady rhythm

Refrain

heath-er.
heath-er. Will you_ go, lad - die,_ go?_
moun-tain.

_ And we'll all go to-geth-er,_ To pull

wild moun-tain thyme,___ All a-round the pur-ple

heath-er.___ Will you___ go, lad-die,___

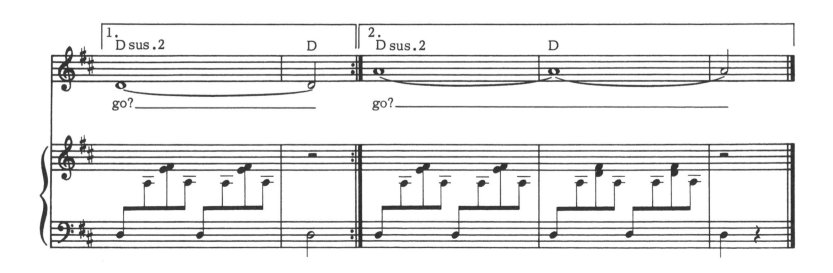

1. D sus.2   D   **2.** D sus.2   D

go?_____ go?_____

Where Have All The Flowers Gone?

Words and Music by Pete Seeger

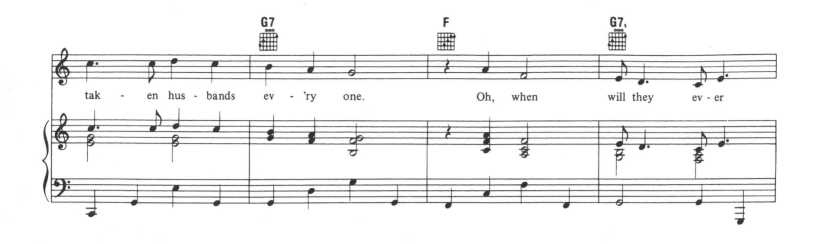

tak - en hus - bands ev - 'ry one. Oh, when will they ev - er

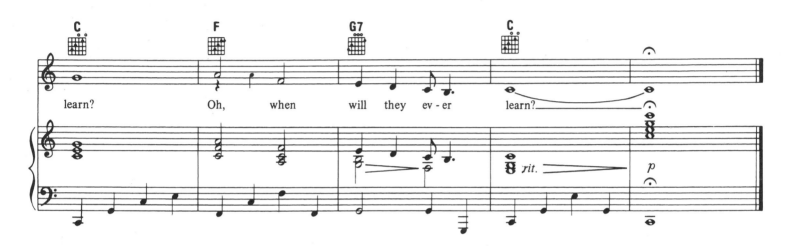

learn? Oh, when will they ev - er learn?

3. Where have all the young men gone? Long time passing.
Where have all the young men gone? Long time ago.
Where have all the young men gone?
They're all in uniform.
Oh, when will they ever learn?
Oh, when will they ever learn?

4. Where have all the soldiers gone? Long time passing.
Where have all the soldiers gone? Long time ago.
Where have all the soldiers gone?
They've gone to graveyards, every one.
Oh, when will they ever learn?
Oh, when will they ever learn?

5. Where have all the graveyards gone? Long time passing.
Where have all the graveyards gone? Long time ago.
Where have all the graveyards gone?
They're covered with flowers, every one.
Oh, when will they ever learn?
Oh, when will they ever learn?

6. Where Have All The Flowers Gone? Long time passing.
Where Have All The Flowers Gone? Long time ago.
Where Have All The Flowers Gone?
Young girls picked them, every one.
Oh, when will they ever learn?
Oh, when will they ever learn?